Deer

Deer

by Christina Wilsdon

Reader's Digest

YOUNG FAMILIES

Published by The Reader's Digest Association Limited

London • New York • Sydney • Montreal

CONTENTS

Chapter 1

A deer grows up

DID YOU KNOW?

- There are more than 40 different kinds of deer in the world.
- A baby deer is often called a fawn or – if it is a red deer – a calf.
- A female red deer is called a hind and a male is called a stag. But in other types of deer, females are called does and males are called bucks.

The baby deer blinks as he looks at the world around him. He is only a few minutes old, so everything is brand new to him. He sneezes as a blade of grass tickles his nose. Suddenly, something warm and wet washes over Baby Deer's face. It is his mother's tongue, busily scrubbing him from head to toe.

Mother Deer came to this quiet spot to give birth. This is her first fawn, but she already knows how to take care of him. Mother Deer licks her baby dry, then lies down next to him. Baby Deer nuzzles close and drinks his first meal of milk.

Soon the little deer struggles to his feet, wobbling a bit on his long legs. Mother Deer licks him with such energy that her baby nearly topples over. But in less than an hour, the baby deer can walk. At about 5 hours old, Baby Deer will follow his mother away from the place where he was born.

Mother Deer leads her baby to a grassy spot in the woods that has many leafy plants. There Baby Deer lies down, curls up in a ball, and flattens his ears against his neck. His coat is dotted with white spots and he blends in so well with the patches of sun and shade that he seems to disappear!

Mother Deer nuzzles her baby and gives him a lick before stepping quietly away. She looks back to make sure her baby is safely hidden, then heads off to find food.

Baby Deer sleeps a little. When he wakes up he looks around, but stays very still. Even though he is very young, Baby Deer knows that lying still and quiet is his best protection from wild predators or gun dogs and hunters. A new-born deer gives off no smells for a dog to sniff out.

To keep her own smell from the hiding place, Mother Deer stays away from her baby as much as possible. But she is close enough to hear if he calls and she is always alert for signs of danger. Mother Deer carefully visits her baby three or four times a day to feed him. Baby Deer leaps to his feet and nurses eagerly, wagging his tail the whole time.

When Baby Deer has finished feeding, Mother makes him lie down again. If her baby tries to follow her, Mother gently pushes him to the ground with her foot.

DID YOU KNOW?

Some female deer occasionally have twins, especially if the they have plenty of food. However, if food is scarce one year, they may not have a baby at all.

Seasonal coats

Baby deer are born in early summer and stay close to their mothers for many weeks. As winter approaches they both grow a longer, thicker fur to keep them warm during bad weather. The mother and her young recognise each other by their special smells.

When the baby deer is a week or so old, his mother bleats softly and leads him away. From now on, Baby Deer travels everywhere with his mother. They feed at night as well as during the day. He tastes the leaves that his mother nibbles and learns which are good to eat. After a few weeks he will feed only on plants and will not need milk from his mother anymore.

Baby Deer also meets other deer for the first time. He joins a small group, called a herd. Young deer are playful, chasing each other about while their mothers feed. They may run after butterflies or stamp their hoofs at rabbits. Sometimes they jump right over each other!

As summer turns into autumn, Baby Deer's coat changes too. His white spots are lost and the colour of his coat becomes more like his mother's.

Mother and Baby Deer stay together all winter. But in the late spring, Mother Deer will go quietly away from the herd to have her next baby. Later, they meet up again as Mother Deer brings her baby to rejoin the herd and her young from earlier years. Mothers and their young may stay with the same herd for many years.

Chapter 2

The body of a deer

The thin, long legs of deer are the perfect size and shape for running through woods and fields.

DID YOU KNOW?

Some deer can leap more than 5 metres in one bound and can jump over a fence 2 metres high!

Leaping legs!

Even though they are big animals, deer can sneak right past you with barely a sound. Their thin, long legs carefully and quietly tiptoe over roots and rocks. Their slim, smooth bodies slip silently between branches and bushes. But at the slightest threatening movement or sound the deer will race away in leaps and bounds.

A deer can run really fast especially over open fields and moors. Its long legs enable it to travel at up to 35 miles per hour for short distances. That's about as fast as a racehorse and twice as fast as the best Olympic athletes! Just like us, a deer cannot run fast on soft soil or through deep snow. Where the ground is soft its hoofs leave heart-shaped prints.

Big deer, little deer

Some deer are very big. The moose stands 2 metres high at the shoulder, taller than a man. By contrast the tiny muntjac deer is only knee-high and smaller than most dogs. Even the same kinds of deer vary a lot in size. Red deer living in the thick forests of Europe are twice as heavy as those that live out on the cold moors of

Scotland where the food is much less nourishing. In America, male white-tailed deer in northern places weigh around 90 kilos, about the same as a well-built man. But to the south, in Florida, the local white-tailed deer weigh only about 30 kilos, the size of an Alsatian dog. Male deer are usually larger than females.

Sensing danger

Deer use all their senses to detect danger. Animals such as wolves and eagles hunt them for food, but dogs, cars and people are also a threat. Humans may also try to creep up on deer to shoot them for food.

Deer are always listening for the slightest sounds. The size and shape of their ears help them to hear faint sounds, just as cupping a hand behind your ear helps you to hear better. A deer can point one ear forwards and the other backwards at the same time to hear sounds ahead and behind. The snap of a twig is enough to send a deer bounding for cover.

A deer is especially quick to see movement. If you stand absolutely still, a deer might not notice you. But just a blink of your eye can cause it to run away. A deer has very keen sight, especially in the dark and its eyes sit high up on the sides of its head, enabling it to see ahead, behind and to the side.

A deer's sense of smell is also excellent. Its moist, black nose traps the faintest scents. Deer often sniff the air while feeding to make sure no predators are close. They also use their noses to smell which plants are best to eat.

Hightailing it!

Many deer, like this American whitetail, have a fluffy tail that they lift up when they are alarmed. This signals to other deer that there may be danger. The underside of the tail is white, making it very easy to see, even at night.

Deer have large ears that can swivel in different directions to detect the sound of possible danger.

Deer often eat up to 5 kilos of food a day, sniffing out the tastiest things before nibbling them.

Well-chewed food

Deer wander far and wide in woods and fields, eating the leaves of many different plants as well as bark, grass, and fruit. They also like vegetables and crops that grow on farms and will even visit people's gardens to eat flowers!

A deer has no upper front teeth like ours, but this doesn't stop it from nipping off leaves and twigs. It simply grabs them between its lower front teeth and a tough pad that forms its upper lips, then pulls off the leaves or bark. Where a deer has been feeding, you will often find stems with ragged, chewed tips.

First, the deer quickly crushes the food with its back teeth and then swallows, sending the food into the first part of a complicated stomach. Later, the deer coughs up a ball of partly-chewed food, called a cud, chews it thoroughly and swallows it again. Feeding like this, a deer can eat at speed out in the open, where danger lurks. Later, in safer surroundings, it can lie down, relax and chew the cud.

The chewed cud then goes into another part of the stomach where a special form of digestion begins, then down through the rest of the guts before being turned into black pellets called droppings.

Favourite food

Of all the foods that deer eat, they like apples best.

Chapter 3

A deer's antlers

Only deer have antlers. Horns are not the same thing. Every winter antlers fall off and new ones grow back in spring and summer. Horns – on cows, sheep and other animals – do not fall off at all.

A fallow buck displays his fine head of antlers.

24

A head of antlers

Every spring, two bumps appear on the head of male deer. These are where its antlers will grow. They get bigger by the week and soon develop side branches too. The new antlers are covered by a soft furry skin called 'velvet' and feel warm as there is lots of blood in the skin. This helps to nourish the growing bone of which the antlers are made.

By late August the antlers are fully grown and the velvet begins to dry up and fall off in bits. This is probably rather itchy as the animals then try to help to peel it off by rubbing their antlers on bushes and trees. By early autumn the bony antlers are clean and shiny, often with pale tips. Antlers can measure more than a metre from tip to tip, but some types of deer (such as the muntjac) have only tiny spikes for antlers, barely 10 centimetres long. Antlers are only found in males, except for reindeer, where females have them, too.

A deer does not grow his first antlers until he is more than a year old. The first set usually has just a single spike on each side of the head. Each year the old antlers drop off and new ones grow. Each new set is bigger, usually with more spikes.

Total points

Young male deer grow a new spike on each antler every year. This helps you to tell how old the deer is. But when a deer has more than about four or five spikes, its age is harder to estimate. A lot depends on how well the deer is nourished, too. Well-fed deer grow bigger antlers than those who have to eat poor-quality foods such as heather. Some types of deer only ever have simple antlers.

Deadly display

When a male deer is looking for mates in the breeding season, he tries to impress the other deer with his fine antlers. Two males will eye each other and if the weaker one doesn't walk away, there will be a fight.

First, the males glare at each other, then walk alongside one another on stiff legs, with their ears back and their heads held high to show off their antlers. They don't charge each other because the sharp prongs on the antlers could cause serious wounds. The aim of a fight is to determine which is the strongest. So they lock antlers and push and shove, usually until one animal gives up and runs away. Females who are watching will stay with the winner rather than wander off to join another male.

Antler drop

In mid winter the antlers fall off. First one drops, then the other, usually within a day or two. The deer then has two raw, red spots on his head, but they heal quickly. The old antlers are not wasted as deer often chew on them to benefit from the nutritious minerals that they contain. Other animals, such as mice and squirrels, may also nibble on old antlers.

Male deer lock antlers in a struggle to see who is strongest. Fighting can be deadly, if the animals cannot untangle their antlers.

Each antler of a male wapiti deer (pronounced *waa-PEE-tee*) can be over 1.5 metres long! Wapiti are like large red deer and live mainly in central USA and southern Canada.

Different deer antlers

Deer antlers vary in size, shape and design. Different kinds of deer grow different kinds of antlers, although many antlers have an overall similar shape. There are more than 40 different kinds of deer in the world.

In Britain we have seven different types of deer. Red deer and roe deer are native species, which means they were here thousands of years ago. North America is home to five types of native deer, including the whitetail.

Unlike other types of deer, both male and female reindeer grow antlers. These have a shape rather like a human hand, with a 'palm' and 'fingers' reaching out over the face. Reindeer live around the Arctic, especially in Alaska and Canada where they are called caribou.

Pretty fallow deer have large flat antlers and are often seen in Britain's deer parks, but also live in the wild, usually in woodland with open spaces.

The moose, the world's largest deer, has huge antlers. Moose live in the USA, Canada and also in northern Europe where they're called elk.

Chapter 4

A deer's year

A whitetail doe giving birth for the first time usually has one fawn. Older does often have two fawns; some have three or even four!

Spring and summer

Spring brings new leaves and grass for deer to eat. The food grows just in time for the females, who are ready to give birth and need to feed well so they can produce enough milk for their young.

All winter, different families live together as one big herd, so that there are more pairs of eyes to keep a lookout for danger. This is especially important where the deer live out in open grasslands with nowhere to hide. Forest deer (like the roe deer and muntjac) tend to stay close to bushes and trees where they can easily disappear from view if danger threatens. They do not need to live in herds.

In early summer, the females go away from the herd to have their babies alone. Later they will bring their young ones back to become part of the herd. On hot summer days, the herd will lie in the shade, panting to keep cool. Reindeer herds will often gather in summer on patches of snow where they will be less bothered by biting flies.

Deer are most active at dawn and dusk, but they often feed at night, too. If a member of the herd is alarmed, it snorts loudly and may stamp one of its front hoofs. This is a warning 'look out!' signal to others in the group, who instantly raise their heads to look, listen and sniff the air.

During the summer the males form small groups away from the females. This is the time of year when their antlers are still tender and growing, so they do not fight or use their antlers at all. They spend their time eating to build up their strength for the 'rutting season' in the autumn. This is when they fight each other to show the females which of them is the strongest.

A strong and powerful red stag stands proudly among the many female red deer (hinds) he has attracted.

Autumn

Autumn is a busy season for red and fallow deer. It is their mating season. It is also the females' last chance to fatten up for the winter before the plants stop growing.

By now, their young are feeding themselves. They follow their mothers, nibbling on leaves and berries, twigs and stems. The deer also eat a lot of autumn acorns and beechnuts. But the males do not spend much time eating as they are busy getting ready to find mates. The groups of males who have been friends all summer now split up and each one gathers as many females as possible. They no longer play with each other, but show off their antlers and try to look impressive and important.

A male deer will often rub his face against trees and bushes as he goes through the woods. He does this to smear special scent from big glands in front of his eyes. The greasy chemicals that he leaves behind will serve as signals, warning other deer that he is in the area. He may also scratch the ground with his hoofs, leaving more scent from special glands in his feet.

These smell messages also help to tell the females where to join up with a male.

The size and shape of deers' legs make them ideal for moving fast, but it is difficult for them to walk in deep snow or mud. Their legs sink in and they can become stuck. If a deer falls on ice, it has difficulty getting up again on the slippery surface, just as we do!

In winter, deer often have greyer and much thicker coats to help them to keep warm. The males lose their antlers.

Winter

By the end of the year the deer have a thick winter coat which they need to protect them against the cold, rain and wind – which makes low temperatures feel even colder. Their thick fur does such a good job of holding in heat that if snow falls on a deer's back, the flakes often do not melt.

Deer are too big to hide in burrows, and in winter when all the leaves have fallen, they have no shelter. They have to live out in the open, fully exposed to the weather. The males may be exhausted after all the effort of the autumn rutting season, rushing about competing for wives and too busy to feed properly. Young deer, only a few months old, may not be fat enough to survive a long winter. By about February, all the best food has been eaten and the plants have not yet started to grow again in the spring. The deer may have to eat dead leaves or strip bark off trees, but this is not a good diet. Winter is a difficult time for deer and many will die.

Heavy snow blankets the land in the most northerly places where deer live. Winter there is then particularly hard. Deer find it difficult to move in the deep snow that also buries most of the plants they need for food. Sometimes they have to stand on their hind legs to reach twigs, bark and pine needles high up on trees.

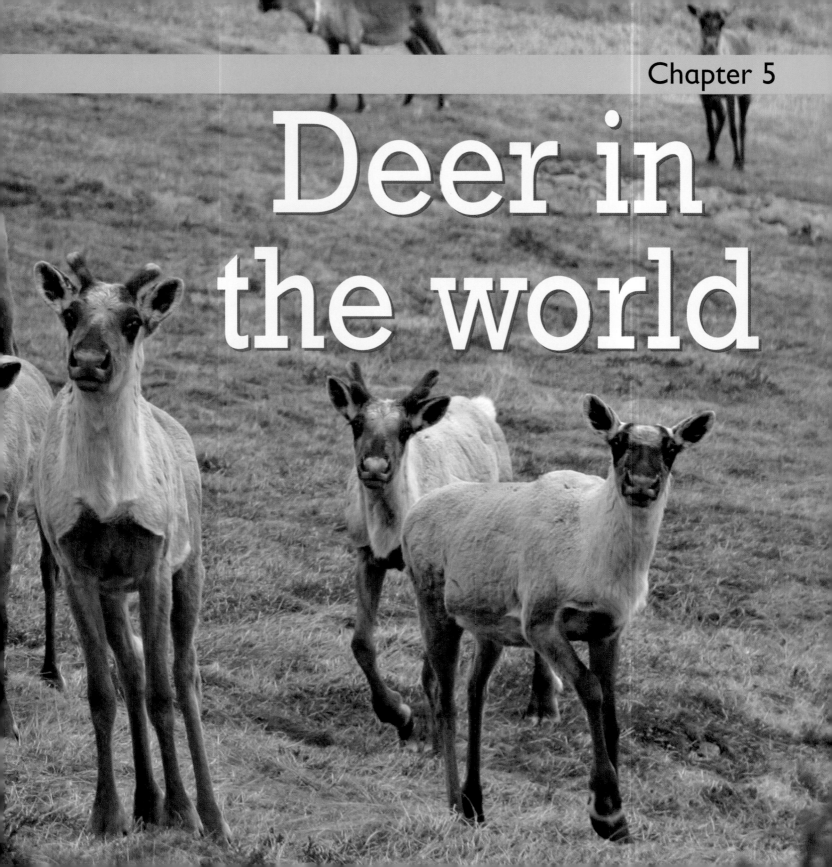

Deer in the world

Where the world's deer live

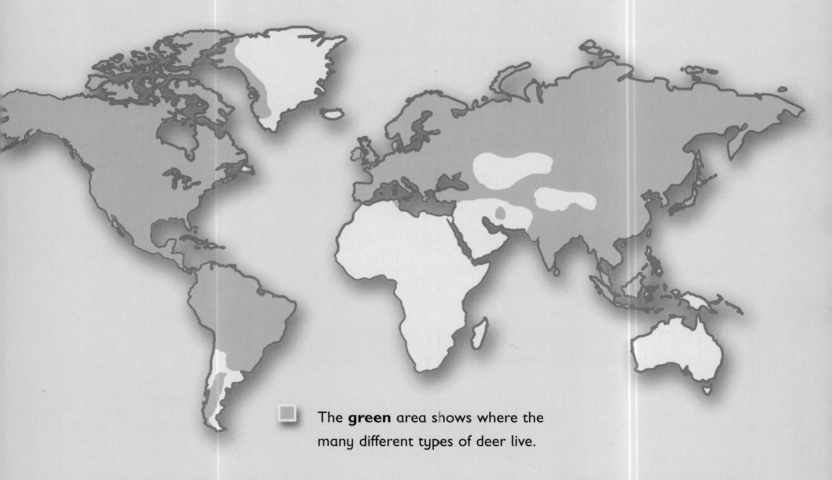

The **green** area shows where the many different types of deer live.

There are about 40 different kinds of deer in the world and some, such as red deer, are found in many different countries.

Other species of deer live in India and South-east Asia, including tiny muntjac. Mule deer, white tailed deer, wapiti, moose and reindeer are found in North America; a few species of deer live in South America.

In Britain, there are seven different kinds of deer. Red deer and roe deer are native species, meaning they came here naturally. Others were introduced from elsewhere.

The future of UK deer

Britain now has more than a million deer – mostly living in the wild, but many also in special parks. The most numerous are red deer, followed by roe deer and the fallow deer originally brought by the Normans. There are also sika deer introduced from Japan, Chinese water deer which escaped from captivity, muntjac deer from India and a small herd of reindeer living in the Scottish mountains.

Most deer are spreading fast and, to ensure their future, their numbers and habitat have to be carefully managed.

FAST FACTS ABOUT BRITISH RED DEER		
SCIENTIFIC NAME	*Cervus elaphus*	
CLASS	Mammals	
ORDER	Artiodactyla	
HEIGHT	Stags (males) and hinds (females)	At shoulder – about 1.2 metres
WEIGHT	Stags	Up to 250 kilograms
	Hinds	Up to 150 kilograms
LIFE SPAN	In the wild	rarely more than 12 years
	In parkland	up to 25 years
HABITAT	Forests, plantations and moorland	
TOP SPEED	Up to 30 miles per hour	

Red deer, Britain's largest
land mammals, are reddish
brown in summer but grow
a thick greyish brown coat
in winter for extra warmth.

GLOSSARY OF **Wild** WORDS

antlers	the bony structures that grow from the head of male deer
buck	a male deer in some species
calf	a baby red deer
cud	a ball of partly chewed food coughed up for more chewing
digestion	how the body breaks down food to use for growth and energy

doe	a female deer in some species
fawn	a baby deer in some species
gland	a tiny part of an animal's body that enables it to make and release a scent
guts	long tubes in the animal's belly through which food passes as it is digested

habitat	the natural surroundings where an animal or plant lives	prey	animals that are hunted by other animals for food
hind	a female red deer	species	a group of living things that are the same in many ways
minerals	natural chemical substances that living creatures need for good health	stag	a male red deer
predator	an animal that hunts and eats other animals to survive	velvet	soft, fuzzy skin that covers a male deer's growing antlers

INDEX

CREDITS

Deer is an *All About Animals* fact book
published by Reader's Digest Young Families, Inc.

Written by Christina Wilsdon

Copyright © 2006 Reader's Digest Young Families, Inc.
This edition was adapted and published in 2008 by
The Reader's Digest Association Limited
11 Westferry Circus, Canary Wharf, London E14 4HE

® Reader's Digest, the Pegasus logo and Reader's Digest Young Families
are registered trademarks of
The Reader's Digest Association, Inc.

We are committed to both the quality of our products and the service we provide to our customers.
We value your comments, so please feel free to contact us on
08705 113366 or via our website at: www.readersdigest.co.uk
If you have any comments or suggestions about the content of our books,
you can contact us at: gbeditorial@readersdigest.co.uk

Printed in China

Book code: 640-008 UP0000-1
ISBN: 978 0 276 44325 1